DECADES OF THE 20th CENTURY

IN COLOR

THE 1910s

FROM WORLD WAR I TO RAGTIME MUSIC REVISED EDITION

STEPHEN FEINSTEIN

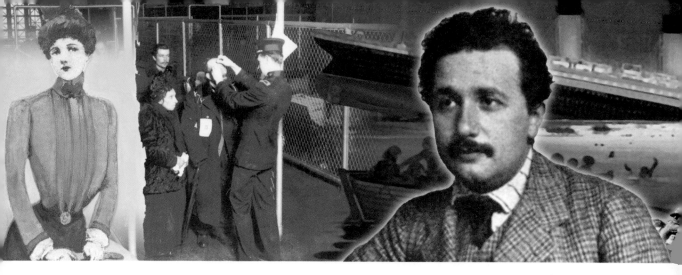

Library of Congress Cataloging-in-Publication Data

Feinstein, Stephen.
  The 1910s from World War I to ragtime music / Stephen Feinstein.— Rev. ed.
    p. cm. — (Decades of the 20th century in color)
  Includes index.
  ISBN 0-7660-2631-0
    1. United States—Civilization—1865–1918—Juvenile literature. 2. Nineteen tens—Juvenile literature. I. Title. II. Series: Feinstein, Stephen. Decades of the 20th century in color.
  E169.1.F354 2006
  973.91'3—dc22

                                        2005019849

Printed in the United States of America

10 9 8 7 6 5 4 3 2 1

To Our Readers: We have done our best to make sure all Internet Addresses in this book were active and appropriate when we went to press. However, the author and the publisher have no control over and assume no liability for the material available on those Internet sites or on other Web sites they may link to. Any comments or suggestions can be sent by e-mail to comments@enslow.com or to the address on the back cover.

Illustration Credits: AP/Wide World Photos, pp. 9, 31 (top), 41, 58; Corel Corporation, pp. 20, 26, 27 (top), 31 (bottom), 52; Enslow Publishers, Inc., p. 11 (top left); Everett Collection, Inc., pp. 17 (bottom), 28; John Batchelor, *Six Titanic Paintings Cards* (Mineola, N.Y.: Dover Publications, Inc., 1998), p. 18; Jupiterimages Corporation, pp. 51, 56; Library of Congress, pp. 4, 6, 7, 8, 11 (top right), 12 (top), 12–13 (bottom), 15, 16, 17 (top), 19, 22 (top), 23, 24–25, 27 (bottom), 29, 30, 32, 35, 39, 40, 45, 46, 47 (top left), 49 (bottom), 50, 53; National Archives, pp. 22 (bottom), 43, 47 (top right), 49 (top), 55; White House Historical Association, p. 36.

All interior collages composed by Enslow Publishers, Inc. Images used are courtesy of the previously credited rights holders, above.

Cover Illustrations: AP/ Wide World Photos; Corel Corporation; Enslow Publishers, Inc.; Everett Digital Images; Jupiterimages Corporation; Library of Congress; *Six Titanic Paintings Cards*, Frank O. Braynard, Dover Publications, Inc.; White House Historical Association.

E **Enslow Publishers, Inc.**
40 Industrial Road
Box 398
Berkeley Heights, NJ 07922
USA

http://www.enslow.com

Contents

The 1910s were a time of turbulence as well as optimism. Change was in the air. Labor unions organized huge strikes. Suffragists (below) marched to demand women's right to vote. Prohibitionists pressured the government to ban alcoholic beverages. And the United States joined World War I.

The decade of the 1910s began on a promising note in the United States. It was a time of growing prosperity. By 1910, America had become the richest nation in the world. As such, it acted as a magnet, drawing millions of people from around the world who sought a better life for their families.

But while Americans focused on achieving greater prosperity, a calamity was taking place elsewhere. In 1914, war broke out in Europe. At first, United States President Woodrow Wilson argued that America should remain neutral. By 1917, his view changed. He said America must help make the world "safe for democracy."

Later that year, while 2 million American soldiers were fighting in what would be known as World War I, the Bolshevik Revolution occurred in Russia. Vladimir Lenin became the ruler of the world's first Communist nation. Many Americans began to fear that a Communist revolution could happen in America. In 1919, a Red Scare (Communists were often called Reds) swept the nation. Also that year, the worst race riot of the decade occurred in Chicago. The decade that had begun with such great hope for the future would end with widespread turmoil both in the United States and around the world.

Immigrants (above) came from nations all over Europe and Asia, seeking a better life in the United States. When they arrived in America at places such as Ellis Island in New York Harbor, they were often subjected to thorough medical examinations (right), aimed at keeping new diseases out of the United States.

People on the Move

As if in response to the invitation engraved on the Statue of Liberty—"Give me your tired, your poor, your huddled masses yearning to breathe free"—millions of immigrants arrived at Ellis Island in New York Harbor to begin a new life in America. Many were fleeing religious, racial, or political persecution. Most hoped to escape a life of dire poverty. For the millions willing to endure the hardships of immigration, America was indeed a promised land. In 1910, the massive wave of immigration that had begun in 1890 was at its height. That year, more than one million immigrants, mainly from eastern and southern Europe (primarily Jews, Slavs, and Italians), entered the United States. Most settled in the large cities of the Northeast and Midwest, where factories needed workers. Immigrants from Asia, most of them Chinese, arrived on the West Coast at Angel Island in San Francisco Bay.

By the middle of the decade, many native-born Americans were becoming alarmed at the huge influx of newcomers. Recent immigrants

After the Civil War, white Southerners produced the Jim Crow system of segregation, which separated the races in public facilities. In 1896, the Supreme Court decreed that segregated facilities were legal, so long as they were "separate but equal." The early years of the civil rights movement, which included parades (below), focused on pointing out the inequality of public facilities in the South.

spoke foreign languages and had different religions, customs, cultural values, and political views. Assimilation into American society was a slow and difficult process for many immigrants. Anti-immigrant feelings began to grow.

Responding to this pressure, Americanization programs were established in schools around the country. Adult immigrants were taught English, as well as courses in American cooking, housekeeping, and childcare. The government also passed the Immigration Act of 1917. This law imposed a literacy test for immigrants. It also prohibited Asian laborers from entering the country, except for those from nations that had special trade agreements with the United States. Immigration did, in fact, drop sharply during the years of World War I (because of wartime restrictions and the difficulties of traveling during a war), and the new law caused a further decrease. Even so, by 1920, more than 18 million immigrants had come to America during the thirty-year period beginning in 1890.

Adding to the explosive population growth in the cities were millions of Americans from rural areas. They, too, sought job opportunities. Among this group were more than 330,000 African Americans from the rural South. An editorial in the *Chicago Defender*, a leading African-American newspaper of the time, encouraged blacks to leave the racial violence, discrimination, and poverty of the South and move to cities in the North. The fall-off in immigration during the war years was causing labor shortages in the North, and factories were eager to hire black workers to fill jobs. Once the United States entered World War I in 1917, even more jobs became available for African Americans. Many blacks went north to take advantage of this opportunity. This mass movement of blacks to the North became known as the Great Migration.

The Ku Klux Klan (above) became notorious for such violent acts as lynching African Americans. Lynching is the act of killing a person as punishment for an alleged crime, without first going through the legal system. In the South, racist whites brutally hanged, burned, or otherwise murdered African Americans.

Racial Tensions

Rural Southern blacks moved to cities in the South as well as the North. Unfortunately, this migration led to racial clashes in many cities. Long the victims of racial discrimination and violence in the rural South, African Americans now faced the hostility and resentment of urban whites who did not welcome them. The National Urban League, founded in 1910, worked to help rural African Americans adapt to city life. The National Association for the Advancement of Colored People (NAACP), formed in 1909, waged legal battles to win voting rights for blacks. It also organized protest demonstrations throughout the decade. In 1917, ten thousand African Americans marched in New York City to protest lynchings.

African-American activism provoked a violent reaction from white racists. The white supremacist organization known as the Ku Klux Klan (KKK)—which had been dormant for many years—sprang back to life with renewed vigor on December 4, 1915, when it was granted a charter by the state of Georgia. Back in business again, the KKK promoted hatred of blacks as well as Jews and Catholics.

In 1917, seventeen whites were killed in a riot in Houston that started after police beat an African-American soldier. Nineteen black soldiers were later executed. The same year, forty-eight people died in a race riot in East Saint Louis. In 1919, twenty-five major race riots occurred. The worst of these took place in Chicago that summer. It began after a young African-American swimmer was killed when he and three friends tried to use a "white" beach on Lake Michigan. Thirty-eight people were killed and more than five hundred were injured in the week of violence that followed.

The Triangle Shirtwaist Fire

Many young immigrant women in America found jobs in garment industry sweatshops. The hours were long, the pay

  The World.

154 KILLED IN SKYSCRAPER FACTORY FIRE; SCORES BURN, OTHERS LEAP TO DEATH.

700 WORKERS, MOSTLY GIRLS, TRAPPED; BODIES OF DEAD HEAP THE STREETS; ONLY ONE FIRE ESCAPE FOR ALL.

Employees Caught on Eighth, Ninth and Tenth Floors—The Blaze Spreads with Great Rapidity—Victims Jump from Window Ledges with Cloth—

was low, and the working conditions were terrible. In 1910, the average American worker earned less than fifteen dollars for working a fifty-four- to sixty-hour week. The mainly young Jewish and Italian women who worked in sweatshops such as the Triangle Shirtwaist Company in New York City earned even less than that. Nevertheless, they were glad to have a job. At Triangle, they sewed tailored blouses on a piecework basis (they were paid by how many pieces they produced).

The owners of the Triangle Shirtwaist Company, Max Blanck and Isaac Harris, were known as the Shirtwaist Kings. They kept the stairway exit doors of their factory locked to prevent theft. On March 25, 1911, a fire broke out. The employees, most of them women, were trapped inside. The only way to avoid burning to death was to jump out the window. Forty-six young women jumped to their deaths from the ninth floor. Another one hundred died inside the building. The Shirtwaist Kings were indicted for manslaughter, but they beat the charge with the help of their lawyer, Max Stever.

The shirtwaist style (above, left) was very fashionable at the dawn of the twentieth century. Unfortunately, the blouses's thin, flimsy fabric caught fire easily. This, combined with the overcrowded and unsafe working conditions of the Triangle sweatshop, made the disaster reported on the front page of the *New York World* on March 26, 1911 (above, right), inevitable.

The tragedy resulted in new labor laws in New York, including a fifty-four-hour workweek for women and children. Fifty-seven laws were passed concerning workplace safety as well as laws covering workers' compensation.

Labor: Cheap and Cheaper

Employers who hired women usually paid them less than male employees. That is why women were hired in the first place. Unions such as the International Ladies' Garment Workers' Union (ILGWU) fought for a better deal for women. But other unions did not try to help women workers. Male union members often saw women as competitors for the best jobs.

Employers in many industries liked to hire children because they could pay them even less than they paid women. During

Because they would work for low wages, children were often employed to do some of the most dangerous work in industrial cities. It was not until the 1910s that serious reform efforts were started to help protect child laborers (above).

the 1910s, more than six hundred thousand children worked on farms. Thousands of others worked in mines, mills, and factories. The work was often dangerous and exhausting. Since its formation in 1904, the National Child Labor Committee had been working to end child labor. Finally, in the 1910s, there was some progress.

In 1912, the United States Children's Bureau was established. It was directed by Julia Lathrop, the first woman to head a federal agency. In 1916, there were still almost 2 million children working in the United States. That year, Congress passed the Keating-Owen Child Labor Act. It prohibited interstate shipment of goods made by children; prohibited children under the age of sixteen from working more than eight hours a day, from working at night, and from working in dangerous places such as mines; and established fourteen as the minimum age for all other types of work.

"There Is Power in a Union"

In the 1910s, skilled workers such as carpenters and bricklayers organized into trade unions affiliated with the American Federation of Labor (AFL). The AFL, under the leadership of Samuel Gompers, was not very interested in representing

Despite the fact that male coworkers often saw them as a threat, women workers (below) became a large voice in the labor movement. In fact, the ILGWU became one of the five largest AFL affiliates by the end of the decade. Labor organization became a big issue in the 1910s. As poet and songwriter Joe Hill wrote in his poem, "There Is Power in a Union":

If you like sluggers to beat off your head,

Then don't organize, all unions despise,

If you want nothing before you are dead,

Shake hands with your boss and look wise.

America's unskilled workers, who made up around 95 percent of the workforce. Unskilled workers were often victims of the worst abuses of the profit-driven capitalist system. Desperately in need of representation to win higher pay and better working conditions, they joined unions such as the Industrial Workers of the World (IWW) and the United Mine Workers of America (UMW). While the AFL was politically conservative, IWW organizers—referred to as Wobblies—often held radical political views. At times, they even said that the overthrow of the capitalist system was the only way for workers to get a fair deal.

Wobblies organized many strikes during the 1910s. In January 1912, thousands of workers at the textile mills in Lawrence, Massachusetts, began a strike that lasted two months. The mills had cut the workers' salaries, which had barely been above starvation level to begin with. Before the strike was over, a young Italian striker named Annie LoPezzi was shot dead by a soldier. IWW organizers, among them Elizabeth Gurley Flynn and William "Big Bill" Haywood, were finally able to restore the workers' pay. IWW membership in Lawrence increased to ten thousand mill workers.

In September 1913, in Ludlow, Colorado, nine thousand miners—members of the UMW—went on strike. They were employees of mines owned by John D. Rockefeller. At the time, the miners were paid $1.68 a day. Their salary consisted of scrip instead of cash. Scrip was not ordinary money. It could be used only in Rockefeller stores and as rent for Rockefeller shacks. The strike lasted seven months. Before it was over, many strikers died. On October 17, several miners were killed in gun battles with armed guards. On April 20, 1914, three hundred guards, some firing machine guns, attacked a miner's camp near Ludlow. When they burned the tents, two women and eleven children who had been hiding in an underground bunker suffocated. Above ground, five miners were killed by gunfire, and more than one hundred were wounded. Among the dead was strike leader Louis Tikas. He had been captured, beaten, and shot in the back. During the following days, forty more people were killed before federal troops sent by President Woodrow Wilson restored order. Sadly, the strikers' demands were not met.

In 1915, six striking workers were killed by guards at the Standard Oil refinery in Bayonne, New Jersey. That same year, Joe Hill, who had been arrested in January 1914 for killing a Salt Lake City grocer, was executed by a firing squad. He had been convicted on flimsy evidence. The forty-three-year-old Wobbly songwriter, became a legend as people around the world rallied to his defense.

Within a few years, the IWW itself would come to the end of its road. During World War I, many people came to believe that the IWW was antiwar and unpatriotic. IWW membership plummeted. IWW leaders were arrested or deported. By late 1918, the IWW was no longer a force in the labor movement. But the labor scene would heat up again once the war was over.

The Red Scare of 1919–1920

In 1919, there were more than twenty-six hundred strikes in the United States. Four million workers— one out of every five—walked off the job. Major strikes occurred in industries from steel to coal mining to railroads. Seattle was the scene of a

The Red Scare led to some serious violations of the constitutional rights of Americans. Led by A. Mitchell Palmer (below) and assisted by future FBI director J. Edgar Hoover, raids were carried out to uncover the secrets of those deemed "radical" and dangerous— including many leaders of the labor movement.

general strike, and in Boston, thousands of police officers went on strike. Adding to the turmoil was a series of bombings around the country. People began to fear that striking immigrant workers were Reds (Communists) plotting the overthrow of the government.

On June 2, 1919, the Washington, D.C., home of A. Mitchell Palmer, the recently appointed attorney general, was bombed. In response, Palmer, aided by J. Edgar Hoover, planned a massive crackdown on anyone who seemed radical. From November 1919 until February 1920, the Palmer-Hoover raids rounded up thousands of alleged Communists, Socialists, and anarchists. Most of these people were immigrants. Hundreds were deported. The Red Scare had a chilling effect on union activity. The labor movement did not fully recover until the 1930s.

Marchers With a Message

Throughout the 1910s, Americans by the thousands took to the streets for a variety of causes. African Americans marched for an end to discrimination. Pacifists marched to oppose America's participation in World War I. Prohibitionists—members of the Women's Christian

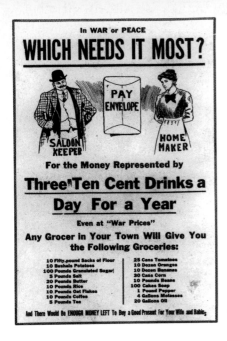

In WAR or PEACE

WHICH NEEDS IT MOST?

SALOON KEEPER   PAY ENVELOPE   HOME MAKER

For the Money Represented by

Three Ten Cent Drinks a Day For a Year

Even at "War Prices"

Any Grocer in Your Town Will Give You the Following Groceries:

10 Fifty-pound Sacks of Flour	25 Cans Tomatoes
10 Bushels Potatoes	10 Dozen Oranges
100 Pounds Granulated Sugar	10 Dozen Bananas
5 Pounds Salt	30 Cans Corn
20 Pounds Butter	10 Pounds Beans
10 Pounds Rice	100 Cakes Soap
10 Pounds Oat Flakes	1 Pound Pepper
10 Pounds Coffee	4 Gallons Molasses
5 Pounds Tea	20 Gallons Oil

And There Would Be ENOUGH MONEY LEFT To Buy a Good Present For Your Wife and Babies

Temperance Union (WCTU) and the Anti-Saloon League—marched to win support for a ban on the manufacture and sale of alcoholic beverages. Their efforts were rewarded when, in 1919, a law was ratified—the Eighteenth Amendment to the Constitution.

Also successful were the suffragists. Led by organizations such as the National Woman's Party (NWP) and the National American Woman Suffrage Association (NAWSA), suffragists marched to demand the right to vote for women. In 1919, Congress passed the Nineteenth Amendment. After it was ratified in 1920, women were granted the right to vote. Casting the deciding vote for the amendment in the House of Representatives was Jeannette Rankin, who, on April 2, 1917, took her seat as the first woman elected to serve in Congress.

Rebel with a Cause

Public health nurse Margaret Sanger practiced nursing on the Lower East Side of New York City. While working with poverty-stricken immigrants, she came to believe that one cause of poverty is families that are too large to be adequately supported. After seeing women die from illegal abortions, Sanger saw the need for a national program of birth control. In 1914 she founded the National Birth Control League and

Margaret Sanger (photographed in 1916, below) sacrificed her personal freedom in the pursuit of freedom for all women in controlling their reproductive rights.

It took only two and a half hours for the *Titanic* (above) to disappear beneath the icy waters of the North Atlantic. The ship's band continued to play as the ship sank beneath the waves.

began publishing a magazine called *The Woman Rebel*. This led to her first arrest because at that time it was illegal to distribute birth control information or devices in the U.S. In 1916, Sanger opened the first birth control clinic in the United States in Brooklyn, New York. Again she was arrested and was sent to prison. But Sanger would continue to fight for women's rights for the rest of her life.

A Tale of Two Ships

Millions of people during the 1910s journeyed across the high seas. For the vast majority of them—immigrants crowded in cramped quarters—the voyage was not especially enjoyable. The ships were not exactly luxurious. But for the other ocean travelers—wealthy families on vacation abroad or captains of industry traveling on business—the ocean crossing was often pleasurable and relaxing. For the wealthy, the great transatlantic ocean liners provided every imaginable luxury. Two disasters at sea, however, demonstrated that money could not always shelter a person from tragedy.

The *Titanic* had completed about two thirds of its maiden voyage from Southampton, England, to New York City, when it reached iceberg fields off Newfoundland. The largest, fastest, and most extravagant ship ever built, the *Titanic* was the pride of Great Britain's White Star Lines. Believed to be unsinkable, it was like a gigantic floating hotel. Among the 2,340 passengers and crew on board were Colonel John J. Astor, one of America's richest men, and his young bride. On April 14, 1912, at 11:40 P.M., the *Titanic* struck an iceberg. Water began rushing into the resulting gash in the side of the ship. Unfortunately, there were not nearly enough lifeboats for everyone on board. A total of 1,503 people died.

A few years later, another ocean liner met a similar fate, but for a different reason. On May 7, 1915, the British ship *Lusitania*, said to be the fastest and largest passenger liner then in service, was en route from New York City to Liverpool, England. It was a sunny afternoon, and the green hills of

Partly in response to vicious attacks on civilians through the use of submarines, such as the sinking of the *Lusitania* (below), the United States decided to enter World War I in 1917.

In 1913, it took Ford workers twelve and a half hours to build a Model T (below). The following year, it took only ninety-six minutes. That year, Ford produced about a quarter of a million cars, about half of all cars sold in America. The average selling price of a Model T in 1914 was about $440, but Henry Ford was aiming at an eventual price of $250. Since Ford's workforce was only half the size of his competitors', thanks to his assembly line system of manufacture, he decided he could afford to raise his workers' wages to $5 per day. Ford's competitors were horrified. This was about two to three times what they were paying their own workers. But Ford knew that by increasing his workers' pay, he would be creating new customers for his cars.

Ireland were visible on the horizon. Suddenly, without warning, the *Lusitania* was struck by torpedoes from a German submarine. The liner sank within eighteen minutes. Among the 1,198 dead were 128 American citizens. The unfortunate passengers had entered a war zone. Within two years, America would declare war on Germany, pointing to that country's submarine warfare against American passenger and commercial ships.

Millions of Tin Lizzies

During the 1910s, the automobile was gaining in popularity every day. Those who could afford a car bought one. Those who could not dreamed about someday owning one. In 1910, hundreds of different makes and models were available, ranging in price from a Sears Model L for $370 to a $2,500 Cadillac.

Car manufacturers also had a dream—to sell millions of automobiles. Henry Ford succeeded in making this dream a reality. He had begun manufacturing his Model T in 1908 with the goal of making a reliable car that was affordable to a huge number of potential buyers. That year, Ford sold more than eighteen thousand Model Ts. Sales of the Model T, or "Tin Lizzie," as it was nicknamed, kept doubling over the next few years. But this was not good enough for Ford. He was determined to find ways of cutting the cost of production. This, in turn, would allow him to lower the cost to the consumer, allowing many more Americans to buy a car.

By 1913, Ford and his mechanics had created an assembly line. Instead of having one worker build a complete car at his own work station, the frame of the car would move from one end of the factory to the other as workers each built one portion of it. Along the way, workers would add axles, wheels, and other parts as the car passed by. This dramatically increased the number of cars that could be made and greatly decreased the cost of building them.

Throughout the decade, more and more cars appeared on the roads. Roadside businesses sprang up, catering to automobile travelers. The first drive-in gas station opened for business in 1913. People used their cars to run errands, to go shopping, and to go to church. Going for Sunday drives and family picnics in the country became favorite pastimes. Venturing forth to distant towns and scenic attractions became common ways to spend a vacation. Picture postcards grew very popular with travelers, who were eager to show the folks back home where they had been and what they had seen.

To raise the money she needed to start up her new Girl Scouts organization, Daisy Low (below) sold a pearl necklace for eight thousand dollars. Through her efforts, American girls would have the opportunity to do public service, as well as engage in activities like camping (above, right).

Girl Scouts of America

Concern for the welfare of children, as evidenced by the new child labor legislation, was on the minds of many during the 1910s. Among them was Juliette Gordon Low, known affectionately as Daisy. Low dreamed of giving America "something for all the girls." What she had in mind was an organization that would give young girls an outlet for their abilities, similar to the Boy Scouts of America, which had been founded in 1910 by Chicago publisher William Boyce. Low wanted girls to have the opportunity to experience the outdoors and to perform voluntary public service-oriented tasks in their own communities.

Daisy Low started her organization in 1912 in Savannah, Georgia, with a group of eighteen girls. Low's "Girl Scouts" were soon happily hiking and camping. Low's ideas spread quickly, and troops of Girl Scouts formed all over the country. In 1915, a national organization made up of the various Girl Scout troops was incorporated as the Girl Scouts of America.

The Dance Craze

Ordinary Americans worked hard in the 1910s. But they also liked to have a good time. And nothing was more fun than dancing, especially to the popular music of the day known as ragtime. Americans danced at parties, night clubs, and restaurants. They took dance lessons, and participated in dance contests. New dance steps seemed to appear daily. The tango became widely popular in 1910 but was quickly followed by one fad after another.

Never before had dancing been so popular with so many people. But while the dancers enjoyed themselves, critical voices complained that the new dance steps were shocking, even immoral. Some critics referred to the new dances as "animal dances." Helping to appease critics was America's most popular ballroom-dancing couple, Vernon and Irene Castle. The Castles described themselves as a "clean-cut" young married couple who made dancing look like fun without being at all suggestive. They conveyed the message that dancing was not only moral, but also good exercise.

Inspired by the graceful moves of famous couple Irene and Vernon Castle (above), people danced the fox-trot, the bunny hug, the grizzly bear, the turkey trot, the chicken scratch, the horse trot, the camel walk, the lame duck, the crab step, the kangaroo dip, the fish walk, and the snake.

From Hobble Skirt to Suffragette Suit

In the spring of 1910, designers in Paris, France, believing they had created the last word in fashion elegance, introduced the hobble skirt to American women. It was very long, reaching down to the ankles, as had been typical of skirts and gowns for many years. However, this particular item was often tied near the hem by a straight band. Anyone wearing such a garment was literally "hobbled," almost prevented from walking. In reaction to the Parisian hobble skirt, in October

1910, the American Ladies' Tailors Association introduced a "suffragette suit." This new style included a skirt that was divided down the middle. Women who wore the suffragette suit could walk freely, taking long, bold strides.

Ballroom dancer Irene Castle played an important role in influencing women's fashion in America. She liked dresses with simple, flowing lines that would leave her legs free for

Although the hobble skirt style was popular for a while, American women, especially those who worked, would soon become interested in clothing that was more practical—more suitable for an active lifestyle. Dancer Irene Castle's startling new styles (left) would eventually lead to the flapper look of the 1920s.

dancing, as well as skirts that were slightly shorter than the traditional style. She wore slips and bloomers instead of corsets and petticoats. And when she cut her hair short before undergoing surgery, she appeared later with a pearl necklace around her head, keeping her bobbed locks in place. Because she was so popular, women all across America began to imitate her look.

Oh, You Beautiful Doll

Composers churned out songs for every possible subject, from romance (above) to patriotism (opposite, top). Both ragtime and the blues were originally created by African Americans such as W. C. Handy, "The Father of the Blues," and ragtime musicians Scott Joplin (opposite, right) and Eubie Blake. Jazz bands were called "ragtime jazz bands," and later, "Dixieland jazz bands" because the musicians usually came from New Orleans. The first jazz band to make a recording, in 1917, was the Original Dixieland Jass Band, an inappropriately named white group from Chicago.

A Nation of Music Lovers

The dance craze that was sweeping the country during the 1910s led, in turn, to a popular song craze. Millions of Americans fell in love with the tunes they danced to, and they rushed out to buy sheet music versions of those songs. Thousands of titles were available in the music stores, and singers known as pluggers would perform songs at the request of a customer. The songs were a product of Tin Pan Alley, the sheet music companies in New York City that hired composers to create the songs. Among the biggest hits of the decade were George M. Cohan's songs about the war, such as "Over There" and "Till We Meet Again," George Gershwin's "Swanee," and Irving Berlin's "Alexander's Ragtime Band."

Phonograph record sales took off in a big way, once recorded versions of popular hit songs became available. In the previous decade, recorded music usually

Those movie actors, like Buster Keaton (above), who found success in the new Hollywood film industry soon became wealthy beyond their wildest dreams.

consisted of classical music and opera. Records now became so popular that sheet music sales were in a steep decline by the end of the decade. The most popular recorded songs were derived from either ragtime or the blues.

A new music, called jazz, incorporated elements of ragtime and blues. African-American jazz musicians such as pianists Jelly Roll Morton and James P. Johnson, saxophonist Sidney Bechet, cornetist Joe "King" Oliver, and trumpeter Louis Armstrong were among the first to achieve national fame.

Another musical entertainment of the 1910s—the musical revue—could be found on New York's Broadway and in theaters around the country. These were essentially variety shows. They consisted of songs and elaborate dance numbers draped around a simple plot idea. Victor Herbert, Irving Berlin, and George Gershwin were among those who wrote songs for these shows. The most famous musical revue was the *Ziegfeld Follies*. It featured the beautiful Ziegfeld Girls and entertainers such as Fanny Brice, Eddie Cantor, Will Rogers, and W. C. Fields. Other variety shows, known as vaudeville and burlesque, also attracted large audiences. Many comedians who would later become famous—including Jack Benny, George Burns, Buster Keaton, Jimmy Durante, and the Marx brothers—got their start in the variety shows of the 1910s.

Hollywood Stars Shine Brightly

The movie industry was born during the first decade of the twentieth century. Most film production companies at that time were located in New York City. During the 1910s, the industry shifted to Hollywood, because southern California's weather and scenery were better for outdoor filming. Major changes quickly followed. Short one-reel films, typical of the previous decade and the early 1910s, evolved into full-length feature films.

D. W. Griffith, considered America's first great film director, produced the first twelve-reel feature films—*The Birth of a Nation* (1915) and *Intolerance* (1916). Griffith developed new film techniques and made use of them in these films, both of which are considered classics of the silent screen, despite their racist messages. *The Birth of a Nation* glorified the Ku Klux Klan, portraying its members as heroes saving the white race from corrupt, dangerous African Americans.

Other movie directors focused on specific genres of film, including Westerns and comedies. Thomas Ince directed Westerns that starred cowboy heroes such as Tom Mix and William S. Hart. Mack Sennett made comedies starring the Keystone Kops, Charlie Chaplin, and other comedians who relied on slapstick routines, wild car chases, and pie throwing.

Despite its blatantly racist message, D. W. Griffith's *The Birth of a Nation* (below) is still remembered as a cinematic breakthrough.

D.W. GRIFFITH'S IMMORTAL MASTERPIECE

THE BIRTH OF A NATION

FIRST TIME IN SOUND!

One of the biggest changes in the film industry was the creation of the Hollywood star. During the previous decade, even the most important actors in a film were treated no differently from movie extras today. They were poorly paid, and movie audiences knew next to nothing about them. In the 1910s, however, film studios came to realize that publicity about particular actors would create a following among the public and lead to higher ticket sales. Soon, American moviegoers were flocking to the theaters to see their favorite actors, such as Mary Pickford, Douglas Fairbanks, Lillian Gish, and Gloria Swanson, who quickly became major stars.

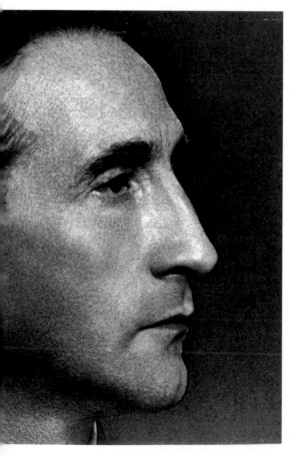

"An Explosion in a Shingle Factory"

Those were the words of an art critic at the 1913 Armory Show in New York. The critic was responding to Marcel Duchamp's painting *Nude Descending a Staircase*. To the untrained eye, the nude in the semiabstract painting might not be immediately apparent. The painting belonged to a new artistic style known as Cubism. In it, people and objects were fragmented and portrayed at the same time from many different angles.

The Armory Show included works by other European artists such as Claude Monet, Auguste Renoir, Vincent van Gogh, Georges Seurat, Paul Gaugin, and Henri Matisse. The works of American painters such as James Whistler, Mary Cassatt, Edward Hopper, and George Bellows

Marcel Duchamp (opposite) caught the critics' attention with his unusual new works. The Armory Show in New York, which also included paintings by Pablo Picasso (left, above), was probably the decade's most important art exhibit in America. It provided an opportunity for American artists, writers, and the public to learn about new developments in the art world. Other artists at the Armory Show were Childe Hassam, Mary Cassatt, (whose work is seen at left), John Marin, Joseph Stella, and Marsden Hartely.

were also featured. The exhibit later traveled to other American cities, including Chicago and Boston. It was eventually seen by thousands of Americans.

In 1917, a group of European artists known as Dadaists exhibited their work in New York. Their goal was to reject all traditional values of art. According to them, anything could be considered art—even a urinal, which was exhibited as *The Fountain*, a sculpture by Marcel Duchamp. The Dadaists, like the Cubists, had found yet another way to outrage the art critics.

Not only was he an outstanding athlete, but Jack Johnson (at right) displayed the kind of pride most African Americans longed for. He flaunted his talent and his controversial relationships with white women, to the disgust of many racist white Southerners.

The Great White Hope

From 1908 until 1915, the world heavyweight boxing title was held by African American Jack Johnson. Many racist white Americans were outraged that a black fighter had the title. Spurred on by the comments of racist sports writers and fight promoters, white boxing fans yearned for the day when a "Great White Hope" would come along and reclaim the heavyweight boxing title. On July 4, 1910, it seemed as if their prayers were about to be answered. A white boxer, former heavyweight champion James J. Jeffries, stepped into the ring with Johnson in Reno, Nevada. Fifteen rounds later, Jeffries, after taking a punishing beating, received a left to the jaw. He went down and stayed down. Johnson was still the champ. White racists went on a wild rampage of violence against blacks. At least eight people were killed.

The next championship bout took place in Havana, Cuba, on April 5, 1915. In the twenty-third round, Johnson lost his title to white boxer Jess Willard. Willard, in turn, lost the title to Jack Dempsey, on July 4, 1919.

"The Greatest Athlete in the World"

"Not for me," said Swedish athlete H. Weislander, a participant in the 1912 Summer Olympics in Stockholm, Sweden. "I did not win the decathlon. The greatest athlete in the world is Jim Thorpe." Weislander refused to accept the gold decathlon medal. "Thorpe won the pentathlon. The medal belongs to him," said Norway's F. R. Bie, refusing to accept the gold pentathlon medal. These two Olympic athletes could not in good conscience accept the medals that had been taken from American Indian Jim Thorpe.

In 1912, Thorpe had become the first Olympic athlete to win both the decathlon and pentathlon. Swedish King Gustav V, upon presenting the medals to Thorpe, said, "Sir, you are the greatest athlete in the world." Thorpe became an American sports hero overnight.

The very next year, in 1913, the International Olympic Committee (IOC) learned that Thorpe had previously earned money playing semiprofessional baseball from 1909 to 1911. The IOC took the gold medals away from Thorpe. In the eyes of the committee, Thorpe was not an amateur athlete, and therefore, should not have participated in the Olympics.

Thorpe was bitterly disappointed. He claimed to have been unaware of any violation of the Olympic amateur code. Prevented from competing in amateur sports, Thorpe turned to professional sports. From 1913 to 1920, he enjoyed various stints with several pro baseball and football teams. In 1950, he was named the outstanding male athlete and best football player of the first half of the twentieth century in an Associated Press poll of sports writers. Many years later, in 1982, the IOC finally gave Thorpe's 1912 gold medals back to his family.

Days at the Races

Thoroughbred horse racing became an increasingly popular spectator sport in the 1910s. Various racetracks around the country began to hold races, known as stakes races. In these, owners of horses paid an entry fee that became part of the prize that went to the winner. Previously, the prize money had come from the spectators' admission fee. By far the most exciting year for horse racing fans was 1919. That year, Sir Barton won the Kentucky Derby, the Preakness Stakes, and the Belmont Stakes, making him the first horse in America to win the Triple Crown.

Not all races involved horses, however. As the automobile began to play an important role in the lives of Americans, it was not long before automobile racing captured the attention of millions. In 1909, a two-and-a-half-mile racetrack called the Brickyard was built near Indianapolis, Indiana. Automobile manufacturers used the track to test new cars they were developing. Races were also held there. On Memorial Day, 1911, the first five-hundred-mile automobile race was held at the Brickyard. The winner was Ray Harroun, who drove a car known as a Marmon Wasp. The race generated so much excitement that the Indy 500, as it came to be called, became an annual tradition.

Public figures attended key horse racing events. Below, a state governor and his entourage are seen in Louisville, Kentucky, on Derby Day. Car racing was a big sport, too. In the first Indy 500 race, driver Ray Harroun's average speed was an unheard of 74.59 miles per hour. He completed the race in six hours, forty-two minutes, and eight seconds.

Although Roosevelt (above) attacked Taft for his conservative policies, Taft had actually been more vigorous than Roosevelt in curbing the power of big corporations, prosecuting twice as many antitrust suits in four years as Roosevelt had in seven. Taft had been Roosevelt's friend and had served as secretary of war during Roosevelt's second administration. He had become president in 1909 with Roosevelt's help. Now, of course, their friendship was over, as Roosevelt helped launch the Bull Moose, or Progressive, party.

Progressive Candidates

The first two decades of the twentieth century, often referred to as the Progressive Era, were a time for reform in politics. Progressive legislation of the 1910s included a federal income tax law (the Sixteenth Amendment to the Constitution), antitrust laws, child labor laws, and the Eighteenth Amendment to the Constitution, outlawing alcoholic beverages.

In keeping with the spirit of reform, Americans elected reform-minded politicians to lead the nation. In the 1910s, reformers from every part of the political spectrum could be found running for office, from conservative Republicans who supported a certain degree of antitrust legislation, to Socialists such as Eugene Debs, who believed that the capitalist system was to blame for all of America's problems. According to Debs, true reform would mean dismantling capitalism and replacing it with socialism, where the government ran businesses.

In 1912, Republican President William Howard Taft was running for re-election. Former President Theodore Roosevelt rose to challenge him for the nomination during the Republican primary. Roosevelt was still popular with American voters, having earned a reputation as a "trust-buster" during his two terms in office a decade earlier. In a speech in Osawatomie, Kansas, in August 1910, he had lashed out against "the sinister control of special interests."

When Roosevelt failed to win the Republican nomination, more than three hundred progressive Republican delegates split from the party. They formed the Progressive party and nominated Roosevelt for president. An energized Roosevelt bellowed to the newspapers, "I'm feeling like a bull moose!" For a time, Roosevelt seemed invincible. On October 14, 1912, in Milwaukee, a would-be assassin shot Roosevelt in the chest as he stood in an open car. He had been on his way to make a speech. Although the bullet had entered his right lung, Roosevelt insisted on continuing to the hall, where he said, "I will make this speech or die!" Roosevelt made his speech. He did not die, but he did not win the election, either. The split among Republicans weakened their party, and the election went to Democratic candidate Woodrow Wilson, governor of New Jersey and a former university professor.

South of the Border

The citizens of Mexico, America's neighbor to the south, also believed that their country needed reform. Indeed, many Mexicans were ready to take up arms in order to bring about change. As a result, Mexico underwent a decade of violent upheaval.

In early 1910, Francisco Madero had sought to become a presidential candidate in Mexico. He was arrested and then exiled by Mexican President Porfirio Díaz, who had ruled as a dictator since 1876. Madero wanted to bring democracy to Mexico, along with better working conditions and land for the poor farmers who made up a majority of the population.

Calling for revolution, Madero returned to Mexico, organized an army, and in November 1910, began an insurrection.

Popular leaders won power in different parts of the country—Francisco "Pancho" Villa in the north and Emiliano Zapata in the south—and joined the revolution, each raising an army. The revolutionaries quickly won victories against Díaz's forces. On May 25, 1911, Díaz resigned from office. Madero was elected president the following November.

But Mexico's troubles had just begun. Madero could not control the powerful forces that opposed him. In 1913, General Victoriano Huerta led a coup against the government. Madero was forced to resign the presidency and thrown in prison. A week later, he was executed. Meanwhile, Huerta declared himself dictator of Mexico.

For the next few years, a state of civil war existed. Zapata and Villa allied with Venustiano Carranza, and the three led their armies against Huerta. In 1914, the revolutionaries overthrew Huerta, and in August, Carranza took over the government.

Carranza (above, at center with beard), a reformer, would eventually revise the Mexican constitution, providing for land reforms and protection of workers' rights. Carranza also became preoccupied with eliminating all rivals, including his former allies, Pancho Villa and Emiliano Zapata.

The Mexican Expedition (above), though unsuccessful, was unique in that it marked the last time the cavalry of the United States was used for a military mission. By the time of the next armed conflict, the tank had replaced the horse.

The United States allowed Carranza's troops to cross American territory in order to attack Pancho Villa from the north. Villa became so enraged at this that he crossed the United States-Mexican border with his troops and attacked the town of Columbus, New Mexico, burning buildings and killing seventeen Americans. He also attacked a train in Mexico on March 9, 1916, killing seventeen American mining engineers on board. On March 10, an angry President Woodrow Wilson ordered General John Pershing to capture Villa. More than five thousand United States troops crossed the Rio Grande into Mexico. They soon returned home empty-handed, unable to find Villa.

Ultimately, more than a million Mexican citizens died during the years of civil war, including the revolutionary leaders. In 1919, Carranza's soldiers set a trap and murdered Zapata. The following year, Carranza was assassinated during a coup by his former general, Alvaro Obregón, who became president. He and his successors carried on the revolutionary ideals, trying to improve the government. In 1923, Villa would be murdered by political enemies.

A Shortcut Between Two Oceans

While Mexico was caught up in the tumult of revolution, history of a different sort was being made farther south. On August 15, 1914, the Panama Canal opened to shipping. The fifty-one-mile-long canal through the jungles and mountains of Panama had taken the United States ten years to build (although work had been done by other nations since 1880). In 1903, a grateful Panama, having just won its independence from Colombia with American help, gave the United States a ten-mile-wide zone across Panama in which to build the canal. With the opening of the canal, ships sailing between the Atlantic and Pacific oceans no longer had to travel all the way around Cape Horn at the southern tip of South America. The Panama Canal, controlled by the United States, would soon become a major avenue of world trade.

Thanks to the Panama Canal (below), a ship sailing between New York and San Francisco would have to travel only 5,300 miles instead of 13,400 miles. During the building of the canal, which had been started by French engineers and completed by the American government, many thousands of workers died.

The Murder of an Archduke

On June 28, 1914, a tragic event occurred in the Bosnian capital of Sarajevo. Archduke Franz Ferdinand, heir to the throne of Austria-Hungary, and his wife, Sophie, were shot to death as they rode in an open car. The assassination, tragic in itself, had serious implications for millions of other people. The assassin was Gavrilo Princip, a Serbian revolutionary. At the time, Bosnia was a province of Austria, while Bosnia's next-door neighbor Serbia was independent. Many Bosnians, as well as Serb nationalists, were opposed to Austrian rule. They preferred either an independent Bosnia or a Bosnia under Serbian rule.

Up until this moment, peace had prevailed in much of Europe for several decades. A balance of power had been achieved through a complex system of alliances among nations. The two major alliances were the Triple Entente (Great Britain, France, and Russia) and the Triple Alliance (Germany, Austria-Hungary, and Italy). But the peace created by these alliances was shaky. Nationalistic feelings were growing stronger, and the major powers were involved in a massive arms race. Adding to the tensions were various unresolved conflicts—territorial disputes and economic rivalries—that simmered in the background. By 1914, Europe had, in many ways, become a tinderbox.

The assassination of the archduke was the spark that touched off the fire. Austria-Hungary blamed Serbia for the assassination. On July 28, Austria-Hungary declared war on Serbia. Two days later, Russia, Serbia's ally, began moving its armies toward its borders with Austria and Germany. On August 1, Germany declared war on Russia, and two days later, on France, Russia's ally. Wasting no time, German troops invaded Belgium on their way to attack France. The next day, August 4, Great Britain declared war on Germany. By the end of August, many thousands of soldiers had already been killed in the fighting, and millions of others were preparing to join the war.

Great Britain, France, and Russia were known as the Allies. Within nine months, they were joined by Italy. Germany and Austria-Hungary, known as the Central Powers, would soon be joined by Turkey and Bulgaria. Fighting spread to parts of the Middle East and even to some parts of Africa. Australia and New Zealand sent troops to help the Allies. In 1914, Japan, declaring war on Germany, took the opportunity to seize German colonies in China and the Pacific.

"The World Must Be Made Safe for Democracy!"

By early 1915, the German Army had become bogged down on the battlefields of France. A stalemate developed. Although casualties continued to climb at a staggering rate, neither side made much progress. The Germans began using poison gas. Before long, both sides were using it.

As the war raged on, Americans were happy that the wide Atlantic separated them from the war-torn European

Trenches (above) were built all along the battle lines, which came to be called the Western Front. People referred to the war as the Great War. Never before had a war involved so many nations and so many troops. The Great War would later be called World War I because the next catastrophic conflict, World War II, would prove to be an even "greater" war.

continent. Most Americans did not want to get involved. In fact, Woodrow Wilson was reelected president in 1916 partly because, as his campaign reminded voters, "He kept us out of war."

Meanwhile, combatants in the war used new technology in the hope of gaining an advantage. In addition to poison gas, armored tanks were used for the first time in battle. New, improved machine guns saw widespread use. Airplanes were also used in combat for the first time—to drop bombs on the enemy and to engage in dogfights with enemy planes. But it was the German use of submarines, or U-boats, that would change the course of history.

Early in 1917, Germany tried to set up a naval blockade around Great Britain, hoping to starve the English into defeat. The Germans announced a policy of unrestricted submarine warfare against all ships entering England's waters. All ships, military or not, would be subject to attack. German submarines began firing torpedoes at every ship unlucky enough to cross their path, including neutral American merchant vessels. Soon, the Germans were sinking an average of six ships a day.

President Wilson was coming to the conclusion that America might not be able to remain neutral much longer. Then, in February 1917, Great Britain gave the United States government a telegram from Arthur Zimmermann, Germany's foreign secretary, to Germany's ambassador in Mexico. The British had intercepted the message and decoded it. It instructed the German ambassador to tell the Mexicans that, if they became Germany's ally in the war, Germany would help them retake the lands Mexico had previously lost to the United States—most of the southwestern United States. The message

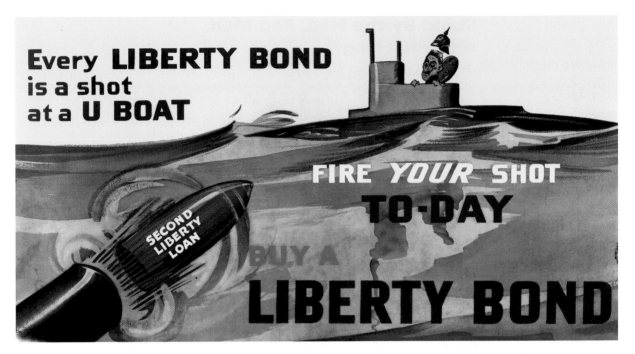

Every **LIBERTY BOND** is a shot at a **U BOAT**

SECOND LIBERTY LOAN

FIRE *YOUR* SHOT TO-DAY

BUY A **LIBERTY BOND**

was made public. Coming as it did on top of the news of several terrible German submarine attacks, it caused outrage among most Americans. Pressure began to build for war against Germany.

On April 2, 1917, President Wilson, declaring that "the world must be made safe for democracy," asked Congress to declare war on Germany. America entered the war on the side of the Allies.

"But I Cannot Vote for War."

Fifty members of the U.S. House of Representatives voted against entering the war against Germany. Among them was Jeanette Rankin, who had just taken her seat in the House as the first woman to be member of Congress. A pacifist from Montana, Rankin said, "I want to stand by my country. But I cannot vote for war."

The government encouraged Americans to support the war effort by putting out posters like this one (above), reminding people of the terrible submarine attacks Germany had carried out against innocent civilians.

"Stand By the Flag, Red Men, It Is Your Flag."

Observing events in Russia during the Bolshevik Revolution (below) was American journalist John Reed. He wrote an account of the revolution in his book *Ten Days That Shook the World.* The event would indeed prove to be earthshaking. It gave rise to the economic and political conflict between the Communist world and the "free" world.

These were the words of Gertrude Bonnin, editor of *American Indian Magazine*. Bonnin and other young American Indians had founded the Society of American Indians in 1911 and began publishing *American Indian Magazine* in 1916. As many as 16,000 Indian men left the reservation and served in the military during World War I. By that time, most Indians were U.S. citizens and therefore were eligible for the military draft. Some Indians opposed the war and the draft. They felt no love for a country that had mistreated them for so long. But according to Cato Sells, Commissioner of Indian Affairs, at least three-quarters of all Indians in the military had enlisted.

The Bolshevik Revolution

In November 1917, for the second time that year, Russia was shaken by revolution. In March, Tsar Nicholas II had been

forced to step down from his throne, bringing an end to a three-hundred-year-old monarchy. Three years of participation in World War I had led to shortages of food and fuel in Russia. The public, now growing war-weary, threatened civil unrest. Millions of starving workers and peasants, living in conditions of appalling poverty, resented the wealthy few. In the capital of St. Petersburg, the tsar's guards refused to fire on a crowd of angry protesters. Instead, many of the soldiers joined the demonstration.

Like Karl Marx, Lenin (left) believed that once the working class controlled the means of production, workers would produce according to their abilities, and goods and services would be distributed according to people's needs.

One of the most interesting military characters of World War I was American General John Pershing (above, right). A staff officer once summed up Pershing's strong leadership skills by saying, "He does not fear responsibility."

When the tsar stepped down on March 12, a provisional government was established under the leadership of Alexander Kerensky. But the new government was weak, and talk of revolution remained in the air. People were still hungry, and they still cried out for land reform and better working conditions. A small group of revolutionaries, calling themselves Bolsheviks (members of the majority), began organizing to seize power. Promising "peace, land, and bread," they attracted many followers, especially in the military. The Russian Army, which had suffered more than 5.5 million casualties in the war, was reluctant to continue fighting. It was eager to follow anyone who could bring peace.

The Bolsheviks were led by Vladimir Ilych Lenin, a man who dreamed of carrying out a Communist revolution and establishing a classless society in Russia. Lenin was influenced by the ideas of Karl Marx, a nineteenth-century German economist. According to Marx, capitalism was doomed to fail, to be replaced by a classless society known as communism. Workers would eventually rise up against the wealthy business owners.

Marx had predicted that Communist revolutions would occur first in the most advanced industrial nations, such as Germany, and much later in nations with more backward economies, such as Russia. But Lenin's message appealed to many Russians. On November 7, 1917, the Bolsheviks stormed the Winter Palace in St. Petersburg, took over the offices of the government, and arrested the officials of Kerensky's government.

True to his word, Lenin gave control of factories to the workers and ordered that farmland be distributed to the peasants. He then signed a peace treaty with Germany in March 1918 to focus his attention on building his new Communist nation.

The War Ends

With the withdrawal of Russian soldiers, Germany now had more troops to throw into battle. Still, the Germans were no match for the Allies, who had been reinforced by more than 2 million American troops.

In July 1918, at the Second Battle of the Marne, the Allied forces, led by four hundred fifty tanks, smashed through German lines and advanced toward Germany.

By now, the German people were fed up with the war. On October 29, 1918, German sailors at Kiel,

While making some generals great heroes, the war also gave experience to the future dictator of Germany, Adolf Hitler (below, beneath "X"), who is seen with some of his fellow German soldiers.

British Prime Minister David Lloyd George, Italian Prime Minister Vittorio Orlando, French Prime Minister Georges Clemenceau, and American President Woodrow Wilson (at left, left to right) are often referred to as the Big Four. Together, they would help shape the peace agreement that ended World War I. Unfortunately, although Wilson was the architect of the League of Nations, the United States never joined. This cartoon (below) mocked America's refusal to join the League.

Germany, mutinied, calling for the establishment of a German republic. On November 9, 1918, Germany's leader Kaiser Wilhelm II, fearing revolution, stepped down and fled to Holland. He was joined two days later by Emperor Charles I, the ruler of Austria-Hungary. On November 11, Germany and the Allies signed an armistice (peace agreement), and World War I finally came to an end.

Versailles and the Fourteen Points

On June 28, 1919, the Treaty of Versailles was signed between the Allies and Germany. American President Woodrow Wilson had earlier proposed "Fourteen Points" for achieving a just and lasting peace. Great Britain and France, however, disagreed with most of Wilson's ideas. They insisted that Germany receive a harsh punishment. So Germany was forced to admit its role in starting the war. It was also required to make enormous payments to the Allies, which would have disastrous effects on the German economy.

After his abdication, Tsar Nicholas II and his family (below) were captured by opponents of the monarchy who hoped to keep the family isolated to prevent them from influencing opposition to the new Communist government. The Romanovs (the tsar and his family) were sent to the town of Ekaterinburg in the Ural Mountains. They were held there until their brutal execution.

World War I, billed as "the war to end wars," had cost the lives of more than 10 million soldiers, more than one hundred thousand of them American. To prevent such a catastrophe from occurring in the future, Wilson proposed the creation of a League of Nations to bring countries together to settle disputes diplomatically. Unfortunately, most Americans feared that membership in such an organization would draw the country into new wars rather than preserve peace. The United States never joined the league.

Whites Versus Reds

Meanwhile, in Russia, as Lenin and the Bolsheviks moved the capital from St. Petersburg to Moscow, pockets of resistance to the Communists arose in various parts of the huge country. A civil war, which would last three years, broke out between the Reds (Communists) and the Whites (supporters of the tsar).

On July 16, 1918, Tsar Nicholas II and his entire family, who were being kept under house arrest in Ekaterinburg, were executed by Bolsheviks who feared that the White Army might free them and use them as a symbol to rally the Russian people against the new Communist government.

Alarmed by developments in Russia, and fearing that communism might spread to other countries, the United States and its allies sent thousands of troops to Russia to help the White Army. But by the time the civil war ended in 1920, the Communists were firmly in control of Russia.

It's All Relative

In 1905, a twenty-six-year-old clerk in the Swiss Patent Office by the name of Albert Einstein had published an article in a German physics journal. It outlined a new way of understanding the universe. In his special theory of relativity, Einstein challenged the accepted notion that space and time are absolute. According to Einstein, motion, space, and time are not absolute, but relative to the frame of reference of the observer who is measuring them. At the time, very few people were receptive to Einstein's ideas. Indeed, few could even understand what he was talking about. However, Einstein continued to develop his ideas.

In Einstein's theory, the speed of light (186,000 miles per second) is constant in all frames of reference. Einstein (below) said that energy is equal to mass times the square of the speed of light ($E=mc^2$).

In 1916, Einstein published his general theory of relativity. He claimed that space is curved by the gravitational forces of bodies in space. Einstein predicted that this could be seen during an upcoming eclipse. On May 29, 1919, British astronomer Arthur Eddington was observing the total eclipse of the sun. He noticed that the light from certain stars was curved as it passed near the sun before reaching Earth. This observation proved

Einstein's theory, which would have enormous effects on science and technology in the twentieth century.

The Lost City of the Inca

At an elevation of 7,710 feet, the city of Machu Picchu sits between two sharp peaks in the Andes Mountains of Peru. The five-mile-square fortress city was believed to have been built by the Inca (an American Indian group) in about the year A.D. 400. In 1532, Spanish conquerors arrived in South America and promptly destroyed the Incan civilization. Because Machu Picchu was located in such an inaccessible location, however, the Spaniards never found it. For the next few centuries, Machu Picchu was forgotten. Then, in July 1911, an American archaeologist named Hiram Bingham discovered Machu Picchu.

Machu Picchu's true purpose is shrouded in mystery. Its houses, temples, and palaces are built of huge stones that fit together perfectly. There are thousands of steps consisting of stone blocks as well as footholds carved into the rock.

Walkways connect plazas, residential areas, terraces, the cemetery, and the major buildings. There is also a huge stone sundial. The Inca are known to have worshiped a sun god, and some archaeologists believe Machu Picchu may have been a religious ceremonial center. Others believe it was a fortress or a palace complex for the royal family.

The Race to the South Pole

By 1911, most of the faraway corners of the earth had been explored and mapped. The polar regions, however, still offered bold explorers an opportunity to venture into uncharted territory. During the previous decade, American explorer Commander Robert Peary had reached the North Pole on April 6, 1909. The South Pole, however, still awaited discovery. It offered fame and fortune to the first man to tread on it. In the fall of 1911, two polar expeditions, one from Norway and the other from Great Britain, had set up base camps in Antarctica, each planning to be the first to reach the South Pole.

A Norwegian explorer named Roald Amundsen and four companions set out for the South Pole on October 19, 1911, traveling on skis and using sled dogs to carry their supplies. Amundsen's group had an advantage over the British group—their base camp at the Bay of Whales was sixty miles closer to the pole. Just thirteen days later, on November 1, English explorer Robert Falcon Scott set out for the pole from Cape Evans. Scott and his eleven men used Siberian ponies and motorized sledges, as well as

Roald Amundsen (below) made history by reaching the last great piece of unknown territory—the South Pole, which had eluded explorers for many years, because of the terrible danger such an expedition entailed.

dog teams. Scott's expedition, however, was plagued with problems almost from the start. Although November was mid-spring in the Antarctic, the weather was harsh, as was the terrain. Before they were halfway to their destination, the ponies had to be shot, the motors had broken down, and the dog teams had to be sent back, as did seven of the men. (These men had been only a support group. They were never supposed to be part of the entire journey.) Scott and four others continued on to the pole, arriving there on January 18, 1912. But their joy turned to bitter disappointment when they learned that Amundsen had reached the pole a month ahead of them, on December 14, 1911.

By this time, Amundsen and his group were well on their way back to their base camp, returning there safely on January 25. Luck had now run out for Scott and his companions. They died on the Ross Ice Shelf when they were caught in a severe blizzard just eleven miles from their base camp.

Drifting Continents

In 1915, German geologist and meteorologist Alfred Wegener published *The Origin of Continents and Oceans*. In it, he proposed a theory of continental drift. Wegener argued that the continents had at one time been joined together in a single mass (which he called "Pangaea") that somehow broke up and then drifted apart. He noticed that the west coast of Africa looked as if it fit neatly into the east coast of South America. He also discovered that layers of rock that matched each other, as well as matching fossil evidence, could be found on both sides of the Atlantic Ocean. But Wegener had no idea how the continents could have moved. It was not until the

1960s that geologists would begin to understand the process of plate tectonics.

Winning the War With Technology

During the Battle of the Somme in France in September 1916, German soldiers were seen running in panic across the fields. They were fleeing from the menacing "iron monsters" rolling toward them. Because they had never seen tanks before, the Germans' fear was understandable. This was the first time tanks had made their appearance on the battlefield. Developed by British engineers with the support of then-naval commander Winston Churchill, tanks were first produced in England in 1915.

Many other technological innovations were also introduced during the war. Both sides were constantly looking for more deadly methods of killing. In Nashville, Tennessee, the largest explosives factory in the world produced more than one hundred thousand pounds of explosive powder each day.

Tanks (left) proved to be powerful killing machines, and the Allies put them to use in the war. While technology contributed to the Allied victory in World War I, it would play an even greater role in future wars.

Incendiary bombs and flamethrowers were invented and hastily put into production. The Germans began using poison gas in April 1915, and the Allies soon did the same. Airplanes were loaded with bombs and were fitted with machine guns for aerial combat. Germany used zeppelins—huge airships—to attack targets on the ground in Great Britain and France. And beneath the sea, German submarines proved their effectiveness by sinking 6,604 Allied ships.

Communication, Wired and Wireless

Many people contributed to the development of the modern telephone—the device has no real, single "inventor." Antonio Meucci, Johann Phillipp Reis, and Alexander Graham Bell are among those who most often share credit for its creation.

Alexander Graham Bell had made the first call, from one room to another one nearby, on his newly invented telephone back in 1876. On January 25, 1915, Bell made the first coast-to-coast phone call, from San Francisco to New York. Meanwhile, wireless technology had also been rapidly advancing. The telegraph, a form of wireless communication, was invented by Guglielmo Marconi in 1894. In 1912, telegraph operators on the *Titanic* sent wireless distress messages in Morse code as the ship was sinking. Ten nearby ships were alerted and helped rescue the survivors.

Within the next few years, it became possible to transmit voice by a form of wireless communication known as radio. In 1915, the American Telephone and Telegraph

Company (AT&T) sent a radio signal across the Atlantic Ocean from the naval station at Arlington, Virginia. In 1916, David Sarnoff (the founder of RCA) proposed to develop radio to bring music into the home through a device called the Radio Music Box. That same year, the experimental radio station 8XK began broadcasting in Pittsburgh. It was soon shut down for the duration of World War I and reopened in 1919. The station received the first Department of Commerce commercial radio license in 1920 and began broadcasting that year as station KDKA in Pittsburgh, Pennsylvania.

A Modern Plague

People compared it to the Black Death—the bubonic plague that had decimated the population of Europe during the mid-fourteenth century. It was called the Spanish flu, because news of the mysterious disease that was killing people throughout Spain first came from Madrid in May 1918. The flu had actually appeared first in China. It spread with amazing speed throughout Asia, Europe, and America. The highly contagious form of influenza spared neither young nor old, neither civilians nor soldiers. There was no known cure for the Spanish flu, which often developed into pneumonia. Death usually occurred within forty-eight hours of the onset of the first symptoms. In the United States, the Spanish flu virus eventually killed more than half a million people.

A French soldier stands before a World War I British cemetery in Etaples, France, during a wreath-laying ceremony of remembrance on April 3, 2003. Nearly 10 million soldiers lost their lives during the four-year conflict then known as "The Great War."

An Amazing Decade

The 1910s were a time of enormous change in American life. The wave of immigration to the United States that had been going on for the previous two decades reached a high point. Millions of new arrivals as well as native-born Americans were eager to take advantage of the economic opportunities the nation's booming industries offered them. New technologies led to more efficient methods of production. Workers turned to labor unions to fight for better treatment from employers, and they were often the victims of violent attacks when they participated in strikes.

In 1917, President Wilson, who for three years had kept America out of war, decided to lead America into World War I. Also that year, the Bolshevik Revolution took place in Russia, and Vladimir Lenin became the leader of the world's first Communist nation. The 1910s in America ended amid massive labor strife and the hysteria of the Red Scare. Many Americans began to yearn for a return to "normalcy," paving the way for the conservative Republican administrations of the 1920s.

Timeline

1910—United States is the richest country in the world; Wave of immigration at its height; The hobble skirt is introduced; **Jack Johnson** defeats former boxing heavyweight champion **James J. Jeffries**; Revolution erupts in Mexico; **National Urban League** is founded.

1911—In March, a fire at the **Triangle Shirtwaist Factory** kills more than one hundred women workers; First **Indy 500** is held on Memorial Day; Mexican President **Porfirio Díaz** resigns from office in May; American archaeologist **Hiram Bingham** discovers the lost Incan city of **Machu Picchu**; Norwegian explorer **Roald Amundsen** arrives at South Pole in December.

1912—English explorer **Robert Scott** arrives at South Pole in January; The Children's Bureau, designed to oppose child labor, is established under the leadership of **Julia Lathrop**; A strike occurs at textile mills in Lawrence, Massachusetts, one of many labor actions that take place during the 1910s; In April, the **Titanic** sinks; **Juliette "Daisy" Low** starts her **Girl Scout** organization; American Indian athlete **Jim Thorpe** excels in Summer Olympics; **Theodore Roosevelt** makes an unsuccessful run for the presidency on the Progressive party ticket; Roosevelt survives an assassination attempt during the campaign; Democrat **Woodrow Wilson** is elected president.

1913—In September, UMW miners in Ludlow, Colorado, go on strike against their employer, **John D. Rockefeller**; **Henry Ford** creates an assembly line in his automobile plant; First drive-in gas station opens; Armory Show in New York introduces new artistic styles, including **Cubism**; IOC takes away Jim Thorpe's medals, denying his amateur status; General **Victoriano Huerta** leads a military coup in Mexico.

1914—World War I begins after Archduke **Franz Ferdinand** is assassinated; In April, the Ludlow mine strike is forcefully ended, killing many people; Revolutionaries overthrow Huerta in Mexico, and **Venustiano Carranza** takes over the government; The **Panama Canal** opens to shipping.

1915—**KKK** becomes active when it receives a charter in Georgia; Striking workers are killed by guards during a labor action in Bayonne, New Jersey; In April, boxer **Jack Johnson** is defeated by Jess Willard; In May, the **Lusitania** is sunk by a German submarine; Girl Scouts of America incorporated; *Birth of a Nation* released.

1916—Keating-Owen Child Labor Act passes; *Intolerance* is released; President Woodrow Wilson sends United States troops to attack Mexican troops under **Pancho Villa** in response to attacks on American citizens; **Albert Einstein** publishes his general theory of relativity; **Battle of the Somme** takes place in France in September.

1917—President Wilson urges Congress to declare war on Germany; The United States enters **World War I**; **Bolshevik Revolution** begins in Russia; Immigration Act restricts immigration, especially for Asians; African Americans march in New York to protest lynchings; Race riots take place in Houston and East Saint Louis; In April, **Jeanette Rankin** takes her seat as the first woman elected to Congress; **Original Dixieland Jass Band** makes the first jazz recording; **Dadaists** exhibit their work in New York.

1918—**Lenin** withdraws Russian troops from World War I in March after signing a peace treaty with Germany; On July 16, **Tsar Nicholas II** and his family are executed in Russia; Second Battle of the Marne takes place; On November 9, German **Kaiser Wilhelm II** steps down from the throne; On November 11, the Allies and Germany sign a peace agreement, ending World War I.

1919—Twenty-five major race riots occur throughout the United States, with the worst happening in Chicago; In November, the **Palmer-Hoover** anticommunist raids begin; Eighteenth and Nineteenth amendments to the Constitution are passed; **Sir Barton** wins the Triple Crown of horse racing; **Emiliano Zapata** killed by soldiers under the leadership of **Carranza** in Mexico; In May, British scientist **Arthur Eddington** proves the accuracy of Albert Einstein's relativity theory.

Further Reading

Books

Edwards, Judith. ***Lenin and the Russian Revolution in World History***. Berkeley Heights, N.J.: Enslow Publishers, Inc., 2001.

Konemann Inc. Staff. ***Decades of the 20th Century: The 1910s***. New York: Konemann, 2001.

Rice, Donna Herwick. ***20th Century 1910-1919***. Westminster, Calif.: Teacher Created Materials, 1999.

Uschan, Michael V. ***The 1910s***. San Diego, Calif.: Lucent Books, 1998.

Wukovits, John F. ***The 1910s***. San Diego, Calif.: Greenhaven Press, Inc., 2000.

Internet Addresses

Russian Revolution
http://www.fordham.edu/halsall/mod/modsbook39.html

American Leaders Speak: Recordings From World War I and the 1920 Election
http://memory.loc.gov/ammem/nfhtml

Encyclopedia of the First World War
http://www.spartacus.schoolnet.co.uk/FWW.htm

Influenza 1918
http://www.pbs.org/wgbh/amex/influenza/

Index